YOU CHOOSE

CAN YOU ESCAPE A HAUNTED THEATER?

An Interactive Paranormal Adventure

by Megan Cooley Peterson

Published by Capstone Press, an imprint of Capstone
1710 Roe Crest Drive, North Mankato, Minnesota 56003
capstonepub.com

Library of Congress Cataloging-in-Publication Data is available on the Library of Congress website.
ISBN: 9798875210341 (hardcover)
ISBN: 9798875210310 (paperback)
ISBN: 9798875210327 (ebook PDF)

Summary: The reader chooses their own path through allegedly haunted theaters, facing spooky encounters and paranormal problems.

Editorial Credits
Editor: Mandy Robbins; Designer: Elijah Blue; Media Researcher: Jo Miller; Production Specialist: Tori Abraham

Photo Credits
Alamy: IanDagnall Computing, 85, Randy Duchaine, 46, Smith Archive, 99, The History Collection, 94; Getty Images: CLAUDIO CAPUCHO, 63, iStock/surfleader, 24, iStock/Willard, 59, Kean Collection/Archive Photos, 90, Peter Dazeley, 72, 82, Richer Images/Construction Photography/Avalon, 29, vgajic, 38; Shutterstock: aerogondo2, 26, FOTOKITA, cover (ghost face), Kopytin Georgy, 56, ODIN Daniel, 103, photorogern, 6, Pixel-Shot, 66, Pupila KDG, 32, Salvador Maniquiz, 100, Sean Pavone, 106, trabantos, 16, tunex, cover (theater), VetalStock, 71

Design Elements
Capstone: Dina Her; Shutterstock: Nik Merkulov, Olha Nion

Printed and bound in China. 006276

TABLE OF CONTENTS

INTRODUCTION
About Your Adventure 5

CHAPTER 1
Setting the Stage 7

CHAPTER 2
The St. James Theatre 17

CHAPTER 3
The Palace Theatre 47

CHAPTER 4
The Theatre Royal Drury Lane 73

CHAPTER 5
Haunted Theaters 101

More Ghostly Encounters. 106
Other Paths to Explore 108
Glossary. 109
Select Bibliography 110
Read More 111
Internet Sites 111
About the Author 112

INTRODUCTION

ABOUT YOUR ADVENTURE

YOU are a student actor looking for an internship. You've been accepted by three different theaters with haunting reputations. Where will you go? And what will you do if the drama turns otherworldly?

Chapter One sets the scene. Then you choose which path to read. Follow the directions at the bottom of the page as you read the stories. The decisions you make will change your outcome. After you finish one path, go back and read the others for new perspectives and more adventures.

Turn the page to begin your adventure.

CHAPTER 1
SETTING THE STAGE

The stage lights are pointed directly at you as you deliver the final lines of the play. The crowd erupts in thunderous applause. Some people give you a standing ovation. You and the other actors move to the front of the stage and take a bow.

The curtain slowly lowers. You breathe a sigh of relief. The play was a huge success! You flubbed a couple of lines during the first show. But tonight, the words flowed through you as if you *were* the character.

Turn the page.

After the play, you ride home with your parents. As soon as they park the car, you race to the mailbox. Inside are three large envelopes.

"Did you hear back about the internships?" your dad asks.

The first is from the St. James Theatre in New Zealand. The second is from the Palace Theatre in New York City. The final envelope is from the Theatre Royal Drury Lane in London. Your future is tucked inside one of these envelopes.

"What are you waiting for?" your mom asks. "Let's open them!"

Inside, you sit at the kitchen table and carefully open each one. You can't believe what you're reading. All three theaters accepted you!

Your parents give you crushing hugs. "Congratulations!"

You text your friend Samantha and invite her over to help you celebrate. While you wait, you go upstairs to your bedroom. You decide to do a little more research about the St. James Theatre in Wellington, New Zealand.

The theater opened in 1912 and was originally called His Majesty's Theatre. Silent movies and vaudeville performances were held there. Vaudeville was a type of popular entertainment from the mid-1890s to the 1930s. It featured singing, dancing, juggling, and comedy acts. In 1930, the theater switched to "talkies," or movies with sound. That same year, it was renamed the St. James Theatre. By the 1940s, the theater added live shows to their schedule of films.

Turn the page.

By the 1970s, the theater fell into disrepair. It started showing movies again instead of putting on performances. Investors helped revamp the theater in the 1990s. Today, the St. James puts on plays and music shows. It is also home to the Royal New Zealand Ballet.

Outside your window, lightning slashes the inky black sky. Thunder booms. As rain hits your window, you read about the ghostly rumors.

A dancer named Yuri is said to haunt the theater. Some say a fellow dancer murdered him. Visitors also report hearing spooky cries. Some say it's the ghost of a failed actress who died at the St. James. Will you hear this woman's cries if you take the internship?

Something moves out of the corner of your eye. You slowly turn toward your bedroom window. A figure looms there. Your heart rate speeds up. The window slowly starts to open, and you hold your breath.

"It's only me," Samantha says as she climbs through the window. "Why do you look so scared?" She's been climbing the tree outside your window since you were little.

You exhale. "I've been reading about ghosts," you admit. "I scared myself a little."

"You? Afraid of ghosts? Since when?" she asks.

Her hair is dripping wet, and she grabs a towel from your bathroom. "What are you reading about?"

Turn the page.

You tell her what you've learned so far about the St. James. Then the two of you dig deeper into the Palace Theatre in New York City. This theater opened its doors in 1913. In its early years, the Palace was the most coveted performance spot for vaudeville performers. By the 1940s, the theater became a movie house. It cost less to run movies than pay vaudeville performers. Live acts returned to the stage in the 1950s. Today, the Palace puts on plays and musicals.

Over the years, many stars have performed at the Palace. Magician Harry Houdini and singers Diana Ross and Frank Sinatra have graced the stage. One of the most famous performers was actress and singer Judy Garland. She is famous for appearing as Dorothy in *The Wizard of Oz* and other films.

"Listen to this," you tell Samantha. "Some people say Judy's ghost still performs at the Palace to this day!"

"But has anyone actually seen her ghost?" she asks.

Samantha has never really believed in ghosts the way you do.

"No," you say, disappointed. "But people can feel her presence."

"Maybe you'll get lucky and see her ghost," Samantha teases. "Any other hauntings?"

You read about other ghostly inhabitants of the Palace Theatre. These spirits include a sad little girl who hangs out in the balcony. A ghostly cello player in white sometimes sits with the living members of the orchestra.

Turn the page.

Samantha yawns and picks up your final acceptance letter. "Tell me about the Theatre Royal Drury Lane," she says.

The Theatre Royal is the oldest operating theater in London, England. It opened its doors in 1663. Fire destroyed the building in 1672. It was rebuilt in 1674 on its current site. In 1791, it was torn down. A new "fireproof" building was built in its place. But that building burned down in 1809. Finally, the current theater was rebuilt in 1812.

"That's a lot of bad luck," Samantha says.

You agree. "It's also said to be England's most haunted theater."

"I can see why!" she says.

Ghost stories have long haunted the Theatre Royal. A man's corpse was found inside one of the walls in the mid-1800s. A ghost called the Man in Gray has been seen where the body was discovered. He wears a long gray cloak, a wig, and tricorn hat.

Another Drury Lane actor murdered a castmate in 1735. Staff say the murderer haunts the backstage area.

Samantha shivers. "I would never set foot in a place where someone was murdered!"

"I don't scare easily," you say with a cocky glint in your eye.

- To choose the St. James Theatre in New Zealand, turn to page 17.
- To choose the Palace Theatre in New York City, turn to page 47.
- To choose the Theatre Royal Drury Lane in London, turn to page 73.

ST JAMES

CHAPTER 2
THE ST. JAMES THEATRE

Your parents drive you to the airport. After many hugs and some tears, you board a plane bound for New Zealand. You've never traveled this far from home and are a bit nervous. But your excitement about interning at the St. James Theatre outweighs your fear.

Turn the page.

As your plane soars over the Pacific, you do more research about the theater. In 1945, Sir Robert Kerridge bought the St. James. He brought stage shows back to the theater. Hollywood stars like Laurence Olivier and Vivien Leigh gave legendary performances there. You can only imagine rubbing elbows with Academy Award winners! Perhaps you'll meet a famous actor during your time there.

You also hope to encounter a ghost or two. The St. James appears to be crawling with otherworldly beings. Theater lights suddenly shut off for no apparent reason. Light bulbs explode. You read about sudden cold spots. The ghostly dancer, Yuri, has been seen wearing a black opera cloak.

Once your plane lands, you drop off your bags at your student housing. Then you take a taxi to the theater. The island nation of New Zealand is beautiful. It has snow-covered mountains, thick forests, and sandy beaches.

The town of Wellington is nestled near the coastline. The St. James is located a few streets up from the harbor. You hop out of the taxi and admire the building. The exterior has grand pillars and arches.

Stepping through the front doors is a dream come true. The temperature is cooler inside. A woman with a clipboard stands with a few other people near the window. They all look nervous. These must be the other student interns. You join them and introduce yourself.

Turn the page.

"I'm Priya," the woman with the clipboard says. "I'm leading the intern program here at the St. James. We have an exciting summer planned for all of you!"

Priya gives you a quick history of the theater. Then she brings you into the main performance hall. It takes your eyes a moment to adjust to the dim lighting. But when they do, you're amazed.

The interior has three levels of seating. Plasterwork cupids, scrolls, and musical instruments adorn the walls. Arches frame the royal boxes, the most expensive seats. All around you see glittering marble, brass, gold, and shades of red. Another student makes a comment about the alleged ghosts.

Priya laughs. "You've heard the rumors?" she asks. "I'll let you decide if they're true or not!"

Priya leads you all up onto the stage. She explains what you'll be doing this summer. Priya says you will clean up after shows, assist with rigging, and help performers with props.

"Oliver, our current director, will run some acting classes with you," she says.

Your body buzzes with excitement. You can't wait to practice your craft, along with learning about how the entire theater works.

Priya's walkie-talkie chirps. "Alright, everyone," she says. "We need extra hands today in rigging and backstage. To help with rigging, wait at the front of the stage. To help backstage, follow my friend Shiela." Priya gestures to another woman.

- To help with the theater's rigging, turn to page 22.
- To head backstage and meet the prop master, turn to page 31.

You move to the front of the stage. Closing your eyes, you imagine yourself as a performer. You can almost hear the roar of an adoring crowd. When you open your eyes, the theater falls dark. The lights have been switched off.

"Hello?" you say, your voice wobbling.

Just as suddenly, the lights flash back on again. The other interns don't seem to notice. Did you only imagine it? Then you remember your ghostly research.

"Are you here to learn or daydream?" a gruff voice asks from behind you.

You turn to find an older man in overalls and a pageboy hat. "I'm Carl," he says. "Head of rigging here at the St. James. I hope you're not afraid of heights!"

"Not at all," you lie. But he doesn't need to know that. You follow Carl backstage below the rigging.

There you see a series of ropes and pulleys that control the curtains and lighting. "We pull these by hand," Carl explains. He gives you a short lesson and steps aside. "Think you can lower the curtain?"

You step in front of the rigging and pull the ropes Carl showed you. The curtain slowly lowers.

"Nice work," Carl says. "Now raise it up. I need to grab some tools. I'll be right back." He steps away as you slowly raise the curtain. It's hard work, and you start to sweat.

Turn the page.

Something moves at the top of the rigging. You assume it's the curtain fabric. But then you see a shape. You squint. It looks like a man! He's walking along the top of the rigging. He must have climbed up the framework.

Your heart almost beats out of your chest as the man topples from the rigging!

Rigging above a stage

- To run over to help the man, go to page 25.
- To find Carl to help, turn to page 27.

The man lays crumpled in a heap on the stage. You feel dizzy and sick. The man fell a long way. He must be seriously injured, or worse.

You kneel before him. He's dressed in a black cloak. Something about it triggers a memory. But you push it away. You have to help him now. You extend a shaking hand toward the man. Your hand passes right through him!

"What are you doing?" Carl asks.

The man on the floor suddenly vanishes. You can barely breathe. He was just here! You don't want Carl to think you're making up stories. You decide not to tell him what you saw. But you think it might have been the dancer, Yuri, you read about. You thought seeing a ghost would be fun. But the experience has left you shaken up and a bit sad.

Turn the page.

Carl says there's a light bulb that has gone out up in the rigging. "Could you replace it?" he asks. "I've got a bad back, I'm afraid. Not as agile as I used to be."

You remember your fear of heights, and this rigging goes quite high. It's taller than your house! Still, you want to learn all you can. You don't want to let Carl down, either.

"I'll do it," you say, hoping you sound more confident than you feel.

• Turn to page 29.

You run backstage and find Carl.

"Help!" you shout. "A man has fallen from the rigging. I think he's hurt!"

You and Carl rush to the spot where you saw the man fall. But he's gone! One of the light bulbs lies broken on the stage in his place.

"I swear, it was a man that fell!" you say. "He was right there!"

Carl rubs his chin. "Maybe it was the ghost of old Yuri. Others say they've seen him fall from the rigging. Don't sweat it. I'll get this cleaned up."

But it looked so real, you tell yourself. Your body trembles.

"We need to replace that bulb," Carl adds. "Would you stay and help me?"

Turn the page.

You nod, and Carl walks away. You're still shaking when a woman approaches you. At first, you're afraid she's also a ghost! But then she introduces herself as Sheila, the prop master. The play has some big props that need to be handed to the actors.

"One of the stagehands assigned to props has fallen ill," Sheila says. "Would you be able to help out?"

- To stay and help Carl replace the light bulb, go to page 29.
- To head backstage with Sheila, go to page 31.

Carl helps you into a safety harness. You carefully climb up the rigging frame. This high up, you see the batten more clearly. The batten is a long steel truss where the sets and lights are attached. It extends out over the stage. You're a little uneasy being so high up. But this is a once-in-a-lifetime opportunity. You won't quit now.

Turn the page.

When you reach the top, you spot a man entering the theater. It's Oliver, the director! He's joking with some of the actors. A couple of the other interns join him. Are they about to start an acting class?

You're supposed to put in the new light bulb. But you don't want to miss out on time with Oliver. As you try to decide what to do, the air turns frigid. The metal batten becomes cold as ice. It's so cold it freezes your hands. Your breath comes out in foggy white puffs. Something feels very off.

• To finish changing the light bulb, turn to page 34.

• To go meet the director, turn to page 38.

You follow Sheila, the prop master, backstage. As you reach the curtains, someone starts booing. Then more voices join in. You stop and look around. The theater is empty. Some of the actors must be rehearsing somewhere you can't see. Still, a chill passes through you.

Sheila takes you to a table filled with different props and costume pieces. She explains the scenes in which they'll be used. She picks up a large, feathered headdress.

"You'll oversee this prop during the performance later tonight," Sheila explains. She shows you how the straps work. It's a bit complicated.

A woman joins you. "I'm Toni," she says. "I'll be wearing that headdress in the show. Could you help me practice putting it on? It's been giving me trouble."

Turn the page.

You grab the headdress and follow Toni. On your way to the stage you pass a dressing room. The door is ajar. A woman is sobbing inside the room.

- To check on the woman, go to page 33.
- To help Toni with the headdress, turn to page 36.

“I’ll be right there,” you tell Toni. Then you gently knock on the dressing room door. The woman doesn’t answer. But she continues crying. You slowly open the door and peer inside.

A small table lamp lights up one corner of the room. A woman in an old-fashioned dress sits at a vanity table. Tears stream down her cheeks.

“Are you okay?” you ask. “I heard you crying.”

The woman snaps her head toward you. There’s something about her that makes you nervous. She seems annoyed that you’re speaking to her. Maybe you should leave.

You can almost see the lamp . . . through her body! But you can’t be sure without flipping on the main light switch.

- To turn on the light, turn to page 42.
- To leave quickly and help Toni, turn to page 44.

You decide to finish what you started and change the bulb. There will be other opportunities to practice acting.

As you crawl forward, something hits your back. It feels like you were pushed! Your heart hammers in your chest as you grip the batten. When you look behind you, no one's there. Suddenly, invisible hands push you again. You scream as you dangle above the stage. Somehow, you manage to swing your legs up.

Soon, the outline of a man bleeds through the darkness. He's standing on the batten with you. He looks angry, like he wants to hurt you. The air next to him shimmers as another spirit floats into view. It's the man you saw fall! He's still wearing the black cloak. Now you remember why the cloak seems familiar. You read that Yuri's ghost has been spotted wearing a black opera cloak.

Yuri's ghost pushes the other spirit away from you. They hover above the rigging. Then they both fade into the darkness. You change the light bulb and safely climb down the rigging. Did a ghost just save your life? You can't wait to tell Samantha all about your eerie experiences.

THE END

To follow another path, turn to page 15.
To learn more about haunted theaters, turn to page 101.

You and Toni head to the stage. You carefully help Toni put on her headdress. It weighs a lot. Your arms shake as you lift it above your shoulders. Once it's on, she makes a few small adjustments.

"That went really well," she says. "I was struggling so much on my own. Thank you!"

She turns and walks out on stage. The crying sound you heard in the dressing room returns. The booing starts again too.

Suddenly Toni screams and falls to the ground. "My ankle!" she cries out. Her ankle is twisted at an odd angle.

"What happened?" you ask.

Toni's eyes are huge. "The Wailing Woman shoved me," she says. "She was booed off this very stage. Her ghost has haunted the theater ever since. She's jealous of living actresses and wants revenge!"

You tell Toni you're going to get help. As you turn to leave, something moves in your peripheral vision. A tall ladder falls on top of you, knocking you out cold.

THE END

To follow another path, turn to page 15.
To learn more about haunted theaters, turn to page 101.

Learning more about acting is why you took this internship. You climb down the rigging and approach the director. He's running lines with two of the other interns.

"Hello there," he says. "Would you care to join our impromptu class?"

"Absolutely!" you reply. He hands you a script page and assigns you a character. Then you and the other interns begin saying the lines. As you read, Oliver gives each of you instructions. It is thrilling to work with a professional director.

Soon, your character has a monologue. You hope to impress Oliver. As you start to recite the lines, singing comes at you from every angle. It sounds like a children's choir.

Flustered, you stop and look around. There are no children here. Where is the singing coming from?

"I'm sorry," you sputter. "It's that singing? I can't concentrate."

"What singing?" Oliver asks. The other interns look confused as well.

Turn the page.

Your face burns. “Never mind,” you say, embarrassed. You start speaking your lines again, but the singing doesn’t go away.

You turn in a circle as the voices grow louder. Finally, you cover your ears.

“Please, stop!” you shout.

You feel cold all over. The voices bounce from one side of the theater to the other.

The singing cuts off suddenly. Priya is standing next to you.

“Are you okay?” she asks. “Oliver is really worried about you.”

You’re curled up in one of the seats. You have no idea how you got there. You quickly explain about hearing singing children.

“A children’s choir once performed at the St. James,” she says. “They disappeared shortly after their final performance here. Some people say they’ve heard them sing. But it’s just a story.”

You feel a little better. But each time you try to run lines with Oliver, the singing returns. You can’t sleep and can barely eat. The idea of a ghostly encounter once excited you. Now you only wish the ghosts would go away.

Priya and Oliver suggest you go home. They think the stress of being an intern is too much for you. But you know it was really the ghosts of the St. James that ended your internship early.

THE END

To follow another path, turn to page 15.
To learn more about haunted theaters, turn to page 101.

You turn on the main light. The woman slowly rises into the air. She hovers above the floor. She is a ghost!

"They wouldn't stop booing me!" she cries. "I was a star! Couldn't they see that? Why did they have to boo?"

She must be the actress you read about. That's why you heard booing earlier on stage.

"I'm so sorry," you tell her. "That wasn't kind of them."

Her face twists in rage. She clearly does not want your pity. You start to back away, stammering an apology.

The ghost rushes at you. You don't have time to move out of the way. You feel a bitter chill as her spirit passes through your body.

Suddenly, you're on the stage again. Only now there's a full audience in the seats. And they're booing you! You look down and find yourself wearing the ghostly actress's dress. You can feel her pain and embarrassment.

Closing your eyes, you wait for this nightmare to end. But when you open them, you're still on stage. You shudder in terror and hope you aren't cursed to live out this woman's worst moment for all eternity.

THE END

To follow another path, turn to page 15.
To learn more about haunted theaters, turn to page 101.

You scurry out of the room and take the headdress to the wing. But Toni's not there. She isn't on the stage, either. In fact, the entire theater seems to be empty. And there's a show in a few hours. This is seriously weird.

"Hello?" you call out. No one answers. You can't find any of the other interns, either.

Someone wheezes behind you. You spin around. An older man stands at the back of the stage. He coughs into a handkerchief.

You're relieved. "I thought I was the only one here," you say. "Where'd everyone go? Isn't there a show starting soon?"

The man tries to speak, but no sound comes out. You take a step toward him.

"Are you alright?" you ask. He might be having a medical emergency.

Slowly, the man backs into the shadows. All that's visible are the whites of his eyes. As you move toward him, his eyes fade away. You step on something and pick it up. It's the man's handkerchief! How is this possible?

You turn to find Toni watching you strangely. You show her the handkerchief and explain what happened.

"I've heard of that ghost," she says. "Some people say he was an actor here. Others say he was the old manager. Lots of people have heard him wheezing."

You put the handkerchief in your pocket. You'll never part with this ghostly souvenir from the St. James Theatre.

THE END

To follow another path, turn to page 15.
To learn more about haunted theaters, turn to page 101.

PALACE THEATER
PALACE
PALACE
BROADWAY PREVIEWS BEGIN OCTOBER 19
ELTON JOHN
TAMMY FAYE

CHAPTER 3

THE PALACE THEATRE

The train ride to New York City gives you time to look up more about the Palace Theatre. A theater manager named Martin Beck built the Palace on Broadway. Beck was already a big name in vaudeville when the Palace opened in March 1913. By the 1930s, the Palace switched to showing movies. The 1950s saw the return of live acts. Stars such as Harry Belafonte and Judy Garland performed there.

Turn the page.

Garland's ghost is not the only spirit said to haunt the theater. As the train chugs toward the city, you read about other so-called hauntings. An acrobat named Louis Bossalina fell at the Palace and later died. Stories say his spirit still performs there. Another tale tells of a young spirit who plays with toys near some of the seats. A ghostly man in a suit is said to haunt the manager's office. You wonder if the Palace will live up to its spooky reputation.

The train arrives in New York City. You take a taxi to the Palace Theatre. Skyscrapers tower over busy streets. You've never seen so many buildings and people in your life. The energy of the city excites you.

A bright marquee sign lights up outside the theater just off Times Square. Lights flash and horns honk as you enter.

A man named Javier greets you at the door. "I'm running the intern program," he says. "Welcome to New York. The others are already here. Follow me."

An escalator takes you up to the Palace's lobby. Golden chandeliers hang from the ceiling. A few other students your age stand near the ticket counter. Javier explains that today, you'll learn how the stage crew works.

"Every member of our team is important," he says. "Not just the flashier jobs."

Javier assigns everyone to a different part of the theater.

"Why don't you join the crew cleaning the balconies," he tells you. "They're still a mess after the last show."

Turn the page.

As you head toward the auditorium doors, a woman stops you. She says her name is Barbara. She's wearing a long purple dress and big red glasses.

"I'm in charge of wardrobe, my dear," she says. "You're the same size and height as one of the leads in the show."

She asks if you wouldn't mind trying on one of their costumes. She needs to mend it, and the actor already went home for the day. You really want to help Barbara. But you already agreed to clean the balconies.

- To help Barbara fix the costume, go to page 51.
- To clean the balconies for Javier, turn to page 53.

Barbara pulls open the doors to the auditorium. You gasp. The Palace Theatre is more beautiful than you imagined. Deep blue seats lead down to a huge stage. The walls glitter with gold and intricate plasterwork.

"Impressive, isn't it?" she asks. "I cried the first time I saw it."

Barbara leads you backstage. The wardrobe room looks like a fancy shopping center. Racks of costumes fill the space. Barbara gives you the costume. Now you understand why she needs to repair it. The neck is torn, and one of the sleeves is too long.

Barbara hems the sleeve and fixes the neck as you chat. When you try it on again, it fits like a glove. She has a few other costumes to repair. You help her with those as well.

Turn the page.

After a couple of hours, Barbara says it's quitting time. She and some other crew members are holding a séance on the stage.

"We're trying to make contact with a famous ghost of our theater," she tells you. "Would you like to join us? It's sure to be a hoot!"

You told Javier you would clean the balconies. But you have always wanted to attend a séance. This is your chance!

- To stay late and clean the balconies, go to page 53.
- To stick around for the séance, turn to page 55.

You head through the doors into the auditorium. The beauty of the Palace Theatre amazes you. The domed ceiling is painted a rich blue color. A massive chandelier hangs from it.

No one's on the first balcony, but someone left a broom and garbage can. You set to work cleaning. You sweep up a few wrappers and some popcorn. But there's not much to clean up.

You're about to move onto the upper balcony when you hear crying. It sounds like a little girl. The last show of the day ended hours ago. All the patrons should have gone home by now. Did someone forget their child?

"Hello?" you call out. "Are you alright?"

No one answers, but the crying continues. You do a quick scan of the balcony. There's no one else up here.

Turn the page.

You look under every seat and between every row. But you're the only person there. You're about to give up when you notice a trail of white mist. You follow it to the edge of the balcony. Suddenly, the lights flicker overhead. A little girl blooms into color. Her body glows faintly. She wears a fancy dress as she peers over the balcony.

"Can I help you?" you ask, your voice trembling. You cannot believe your eyes. It's the ghostly girl you read about!

She tells you she can't find her little brother. "Will you help me find him?" the girl asks.

Just then, Javier enters the auditorium from the stage. You suddenly realize you should be done with your work. There's still time to clean the upper balcony before he notices.

- To ignore the ghost and finish cleaning, turn to page 60.
- To help the ghostly girl find her brother, turn to page 70.

The next show isn't until tomorrow afternoon. You can clean the balconies first thing in the morning.

You follow Barbara to the stage. A round table sits at its center. A black tablecloth is draped over it. Candles flicker. You and Barbara take the remaining empty chairs.

The medium is a woman with long black hair. She explains how the séance is going to work. She's going to try to summon the ghost of Louis Bossalina. He was an acrobat who performed at the Palace. During a show in 1935, he fell and was injured. He didn't die in the theater, but his spirit lingers.

"Before we begin, I have a warning," the medium says. "Keep your eyes shut at all times. Looking at Bossalina's ghost can bring bad luck. Even death."

Turn the page.

You shudder. Barbara leans over and tells you it's all for fun. But you're not so sure.

"Let us join hands," the medium instructs. You clasp hands with Barbara and another intern. The medium begins chanting something in a low voice. Your pulse drums in your throat.

Suddenly, the table lifts slightly off the floor. Your eyes snap open. No one else seems concerned as it hovers there.

- To continue with the séance, go to page 57.
- To leave and run away, turn to page 58.

You remember the medium's warning. Looking at this ghost could cause bad luck, or worse. You clamp your eyes shut, afraid to see anything else.

The table continues to float. Your palms sweat. Your heart races. The séance doesn't feel fun anymore. Maybe you should have gone to sweep the balconies. But you don't want everyone to know how afraid you are, so you stay put.

A bloodcurdling scream rips through the silent theater. The table lands with a thud. You forget the medium's warning and open your eyes. A man falls from a tightrope strung overhead. He crashes onto some seats in the audience.

You look around the table. No one else's eyes are open. Have you just cursed yourself?

- To shut your eyes again, turn to page 62.
- To help the man, turn to page 64.

You push back your chair and run from the table. Your heart pounds. You hurry down the steps into the rows of seats.

"Wait!" the medium shouts. "Come back!"

You ignore her. You're almost at the lobby doors when you hear faint singing. The sound seems to be coming from the back of the auditorium. You stop. It's a woman's voice. And it sounds vaguely familiar.

You move toward the sound of the woman singing. It seems to be coming from a small door at the back of the room. It grows louder the closer you get.

You stop in front of the door. The singing is coming from the other side. The voice is beautiful. When you reach out to open it, the hairs on your neck stand up.

Something tells you not to open the door. But her voice is almost . . . calling you.

- To open the door, turn to page 67.
- To leave the theater, turn to page 68.

You back away from the ghostly girl. You probably can't help her anyway. You don't want to let Javier down on the first day. As you start to turn, the ghost fades away. You finish cleaning and dump the trash outside.

When you return, the once-empty lobby is bustling with people. They wear tuxedos and fancy dresses from another time period. You're baffled. There isn't supposed to be another show today. And the scene makes you feel somewhat out of place. No one dresses like this anymore.

You feel strange doing so, but you tap the shoulder of a man wearing a top hat.

"Excuse me, but could you tell me what year it is?" you ask.

"It's nineteen thirty-five," he says in a foreign accent. The man gives you a strange look.

You shake your head. That's nearly one hundred years ago!

Suddenly, the crying returns. You dash into the auditorium and up to the balcony. There, you find the ghostly girl. She's still looking down at the crowd. Now patrons fill every seat, laughing and talking. The walls feel like they're closing in on you.

The girl turns and looks at you. "Why wouldn't you help me?" she asks. Your blood runs cold, and you stumble backward into one of the seats.

You suddenly find yourself alone in the empty auditorium. You are still holding the broom. The girl is gone. The next time a Palace spirit reaches out to you, you'll listen.

THE END

To follow another path, turn to page 15.
To learn more about haunted theaters, turn to page 101.

No one saw you look at the ghost of the acrobat. Besides, curses aren't real, are they? You close your eyes and take a deep breath.

"It is safe to open your eyes now," the medium says when the séance ends.

When you open your eyes, she's looking right at you. Does she know you peeked?

You and Barbara leave the theater together. Barbara chats excitedly about the séance. She admits she almost opened her eyes.

"You didn't open yours, did you?" she teases.

You laugh nervously and say no. Your first day at the Palace was one to remember. Now you need a good night's sleep.

When you step off the curb, Barbara shouts your name. But it's too late—a bus hits you. The image of Louis Bossalina falling is the last thing you remember.

THE END

To follow another path, turn to page 15.

To learn more about haunted theaters, turn to page 101.

You can't tell if the man who fell is a ghost or not. You quickly scoot back from the table.

"Wait!" the medium shouts. "It's not safe!" You ignore her and race to where the man fell. His back is twisted in an unnatural angle. You might be too late.

The closer you get, the more unsettled you feel. You can see through his body to the deep blue of the chairs. He flickers and slowly dissolves away.

It was a ghost!

Someone taps your shoulder, and you spin around. It's Louis Bossalina, the man who fell! He's smiling.

"Would you like to join my show?" he asks.

"No," you manage to squeak out, terrified.

But he reaches out and grabs your hand. Suddenly, the theater is lit up and filled with audience members. They're wearing clothing from the 1930s. The séance members are gone.

A breeze wraps around you, and your stomach lurches. You're up on a trapeze platform! Louis stands on a platform opposite you. He points a ghostly finger in your direction. He wants you to perform a stunt with him!

You shake your head no, but your body moves anyway. You hook your knees over the trapeze bar and swing in the direction of Louis. You extend your arms, ready to catch him as he swings toward you.

You watch helplessly as Louis slips from your grip. He plummets onto the audience below. People scream. You close your eyes, hoping to wake up from this nightmare.

Turn the page.

Suddenly, you're back in your bedroom at home. Samantha is holding the acceptance letters for the internships.

"The Palace sounds amazing," she says. "You should totally go there!"

"The Palace is out," you say and toss the letter in the trash.

THE END

To follow another path, turn to page 15.
To learn more about haunted theaters, turn to page 101.

Curiosity wins out, and you open the door. The face of a woman slowly materializes. She has short dark hair and big brown eyes. You've seen her face before. It's Hollywood legend Judy Garland! You can't believe the ghost story is actually true.

You try to speak to her. But you seem to have lost your voice. When Judy smiles, you grow dizzy and faint. When you wake up, Barbara and the others surround you.

"I saw Judy," you tell them. "She was here!"

"I've heard her singing from behind that door," Barbara tells you. "But I've never seen her. You're so lucky!"

THE END

To follow another path, turn to page 15.
To learn more about haunted theaters, turn to page 101.

You dash out of the auditorium and burst into the lobby. A janitor asks you if you're okay, but you keep running.

Outside, you hail a cab and return to your student lodging. You're not sure an internship at the Palace Theatre is right for you.

You were so excited to work at a haunted theater. But the experience has left you shaken. Maybe a good night's sleep will help you decide. You climb into bed and fall into a dreamless sleep.

The next morning, you feel much better. You decide you were overreacting and return to the theater. You work hard and become one of the best interns the Palace has ever had.

You get into a top drama school. After college, you sing one of Judy Garland's songs at an audition. You get the part! Critics and audiences love your performance. Soon, you become a star of the stage.

After many years, you return to the Palace Theatre for your final show before you retire. For your encore song, you sing Garland's "Somewhere Over the Rainbow."

You lock eyes with a woman in the audience. She's almost . . . glowing. It's Judy's ghost! She smiles at you before fading away.

THE END

To follow another path, turn to page 15.
To learn more about haunted theaters, turn to page 101.

"Of course I'll help," you tell the girl. Maybe then her restless spirit won't be trapped at the Palace Theatre.

She floats toward you. Her hair hovers around her face as if she's underwater. She holds out a hand.

You put your hand in hers. You can almost feel it! But it's mostly cold air. The girl leads you around the balcony. You've already cleaned this level. Still, you keep your eyes open for a little boy.

Near the back of the balcony, something flickers on the floor. It's the boy! He plays with toy trucks. His body fades in and out.

"Hello there," you say quietly. "I have someone who's been searching for you." The boy looks up. The little ghost girl wraps him up in a big hug.

"Thank you," she says as they disappear together.

That night, you return to your lodging, exhausted but glad you could help. In the morning, there's a small toy truck on your bedside table. You smile as you hold it to your heart.

THE END

To follow another path, turn to page 15.

To learn more about haunted theaters, turn to page 101.

THEATRE ROYAL DRURY LANE

CHAPTER 4

THE THEATRE ROYAL DRURY LANE

You pack your bags and catch a flight to London, England. Your journey is the perfect chance to learn more about the Theatre Royal Drury Lane. You settle into your seat and begin reading.

Playwright Thomas Killigrew began the theater for his company of actors. He was given a royal charter from King Charles II to build it. The theater opened on May 7, 1663. The building burned down in 1672. It was rebuilt in 1674 on Drury Lane.

Turn the page.

Over the years, Drury Lane has put on famous shows, from *My Fair Lady* to *Frozen: The Musical*. The theater has also had famous visitors. Many of England's kings and queens have attended performances there. In 1800, someone tried to shoot King George III at the theater. The king was fine and insisted the show go on. In 1947, Queen Elizabeth II saw *Oklahoma!* there when she was still a princess.

Not all the drama at the Theatre Royal Drury Lane happens on the stage. Many believe it to be England's most haunted theater. Some say it's the most haunted theater on Earth. In 1848, workers discovered a small room behind one of the walls. Inside, they found a skeleton. Police were unable to identify the body.

Since the 1930s, a ghost dressed in gray has been spotted near this wall. Some believe it's the ghost of the man found there. Others say the ghost is that of Thomas Hallam. In 1735, a fellow actor killed Hallam at the theater. With all that history, you can understand how the theater got its haunting reputation.

After your plane lands, you catch a bus to the theater. The bus takes you past Buckingham Palace and Westminster Abbey. Big Ben chimes over the capital city. You can't wait to explore.

Finally, the bus stops in front of the Theatre Royal Drury Lane. You look up at the plaster and brick building. It's a bit plain. But when you step through the doors, your jaw drops.

Turn the page.

The interior of the Drury Lane sparkles and shines. You can almost see your reflection in the marble floors. Huge open staircases run up to each floor. Statues adorn the walls. This theater looks fit for royalty.

You're so busy admiring the space, you accidentally back into someone. "I'm sorry," you say as you turn around. But no one's there.

A young man approaches you. "Seen a ghost, have you?" he asks. He can't be much older than you are.

"I'm not sure," you tell him. You introduce yourself. "I'm here for the summer intern program."

He shakes your hand. He tells you his name is Hugh. He's an intern too.

“But that’s not entirely why I’m here,” he admits. “I’m a ghost-hunter! I run my own podcast too.”

Hugh grew up in London. His grandmother used to take him here when he was a kid. “Once, a ghost knocked her hat clean off her head!”

Hugh takes a small device out of his bag. He says it’s an EMF meter that can find changes in the electromagnetic field. It flashes when it senses ghostly activity. He also has a digital thermometer to find cold spots.

“We’re early, so I’m going to snoop around a bit,” Hugh says. “Want to join me on my ghost hunt?”

Turn the page.

Exploring the theater to look for ghosts does sound like fun. Plus, it will give you the chance to get to know Hugh better. You're about to accept the invitation when you notice a man across the lobby.

The man wears a fancy gray suit. He slowly waves at you and Hugh. This must be Archie. He oversees the intern program. You spoke on the phone, and he sounded very friendly. But this man has a scowl on his face.

- To hunt for ghosts with Hugh, go to page 79.
- To check in with Archie, turn to page 82.

The man in gray gives you an uneasy feeling. You're not supposed to meet up with Archie for another hour. And he told you to meet him inside the auditorium, not the lobby. You decide to go with Hugh.

"Let's go find a ghost!" you tell Hugh.

When you look back, the man in gray is gone. Together, you and Hugh roam the rambling old theater. It's recently been renovated. Every room looks like it belongs in a palace.

You pass by an old oil painting of a woman and stop. "Look at this," you tell Hugh.

A plaque under the painting says the woman is Sarah Siddons. She was an actress at the theater in the 1700s. The hairs on your neck stand up.

Turn the page.

There's something strange about this painting. For a second, you think you see her eyes follow you as you move away.

"This way," Hugh says, beckoning you to walk with him.

You slip past security and head backstage. You're near some dressing rooms when Hugh nudges you. His EMF meter is flashing. Hugh moves the device toward one of the dressing room doors. It flashes faster and faster.

"There's something otherworldly in there," Hugh whispers.

The air grows colder. His digital thermometer says the temperature has dropped ten degrees.

"But the door's closed," you say. "We probably shouldn't open it."

Hugh shrugs. "I need to see if there are any ghosts. You coming or not?"

As you try to decide what to do, a woman turns down the hall. She looks familiar. The woman holds a clipboard and wears a headset around her neck. She stops and points at you.

"I need a couple of extras on stage to help block this scene," she says. Then she disappears around the corner.

"That's Madeline, the show's director!" Hugh says. "She's wicked famous."

You've heard of Madeline too. She directed some of your favorite shows. You're curious about what is on the other side of the door. But now would be the perfect opportunity to introduce yourself to Madeline.

- To go into the dressing room with Hugh, turn to page 84.
- To introduce yourself to Madeline, turn to page 86.

You tell Hugh good luck and cross the lobby. You introduce yourself to Archie. He doesn't respond. "I'm one of the summer interns," you add. "We spoke on the phone."

Instead of greeting you, Archie motions for you to follow him. You're a little put off but trail him into the auditorium.

The interior of the Theatre Royal Drury Lane

The seating area of the Drury Lane takes your breath away. Deep crimson seats lead to the massive stage. Golden plasterwork and lavish box seats surround you.

Archie leads you to one of the balconies. He stops next to a blank wall. Then he turns to you and points at the wall. You wait for him to explain himself. But he won't speak.

"I don't understand what you want me to do," you tell him. But he just keeps pointing at the wall. It makes no sense. You're starting to think this isn't Archie at all.

"Are you Archie?" you ask, your voice shaking.

He doesn't answer.

- To approach the wall anyway, turn to page 92.
- To go backstage and find someone else in charge, turn to page 88.

Hugh slowly turns the handle on the dressing room door. As he pushes it open, the hinges creak. You swallow down your fear.

Inside, the room is dimly lit. It has an earthy smell, like rotting leaves. A woman in a period costume sits at a vanity table. She's combing her hair. She wears a large hat with black feathers.

A sense of dread slithers up your spine. You know you've seen her before. But when and where?

Hugh leans close to you. "She looks familiar," he whispers. His voice shakes. "I don't think she's in the show."

Then you realize where you've seen her. It's the woman from the painting, Sarah Siddons!

Hugh hands you his camera and asks you to take a photo. Then he slowly steps closer to the ghost. You try to work the camera, but your hands won't stop shaking. You can't seem to find the right button.

Suddenly, the ghost rises from the chair. Her skirt billows in and out, as if a breeze blows. But the air is completely still. She drifts toward you. Her feet don't touch the ground.

Sarah Siddons

- To stay and try to capture the ghost on film, turn to page 91.
- To run away and be an extra, turn to 86.

You run to the stage to be an extra! There are a few other interns already there. Madeline, the director, is speaking to one of them. When they finish talking, you introduce yourself.

"Welcome to Drury Lane," Madeline says. "Would you mind standing over there?" She points to the front of the stage.

You move to the spot Madeline chose. You can't believe you just met a famous director! You look out at the empty seats. Maybe one day you'll perform on this very stage.

"No, over there!" the director yells in your direction.

She seems a bit annoyed. You don't want to let her down. But you're not sure where you're supposed to stand.

Suddenly, two hands grip your upper arms. You twist around, but no one's there. The invisible hands gently guide you downstage a few feet. Then the pressure goes away.

The director gives you a thumbs-up. Did you just get help from a ghost? You're starting to get a strange feeling. You don't feel completely safe.

- To hide backstage, turn to page 88.
- To stay where you are, turn to page 89.

You hurry backstage. Stagehands scurry about. They work on set pieces, rigging, and wardrobes. Watching them work calms you down.

You soon notice an actor pacing in the hall. He's tall, thin, and carries a cane. He looks upset, and he's muttering to himself.

You've been nervous before a show plenty of times. Maybe you could help him run his lines. That might help him feel better.

As you approach the actor, two stagehands bump into each other. One of them drops a large stack of playbills. The papers go flying across the floor like huge snowflakes.

- To approach the nervous actor, turn to page 94.
- To help pick up the playbills, go to page 97.

You stay where you are and wait for more instructions. You don't want to cause a scene your first day here. One of the stagehands pushes a large mirror behind you.

As they pass by, you catch your reflection in the mirror. Only you're not alone. A man wearing white clown makeup stands directly behind you. And he's grinning at you.

You scream and spin around. But the clown is gone.

"What's going on?" Madeline asks.

"I saw . . . a clown . . . in the reflection," you admit. "He was standing right behind me."

When you were young, you got lost at a circus. You have been afraid of clowns ever since.

Turn the page.

Joseph Grimaldi

Madeline rushes over to you. “That sounds like Joseph Grimaldi’s ghost,” she says. “He performed at the Drury Lane as a clown in the 1700s and 1800s. Just ignore him. He’s harmless.”

Ignore a clown ghost? You can’t do that. You hurry out of the theater and never look back. No internship is worth sharing the stage with a ghostly clown.

THE END

To follow another path, turn to page 15.
To learn more about haunted theaters, turn to page 101.

The ghostly Sarah Siddons hovers just in front of you. Her body is transparent. You can barely breathe.

You aim the camera and snap a photo. The flash brightens the room instantly. When the light fades, the ghost of Sarah Siddons is gone.

"Where did she go?" Hugh asks. He takes his camera and quickly looks through the images. "There's nothing here." His shoulders slump. He's clearly disappointed.

"We should go," you say.

Hugh nods, but then he looks at you. His eyes go wide. He reaches out and pulls something from your hair. It's a large black feather.

THE END

To follow another path, turn to page 15.

To learn more about haunted theaters, turn to page 101.

Does he want you to touch the wall? It could be a rite of passage at the Theatre Royal Drury Lane. If this is a test, you want to pass it.

You reach your shaking hand forward to touch the wall. The moment your fingers graze it, the wall changes. Some of the boards have been removed. And there are men in construction gear and scaffolding. They weren't there a minute ago.

"I found something!" one of the men shouts.

You move closer for a better look. There's a skeleton lying inside a small room. A dagger sticks out from its ribs. Pieces of tattered gray fabric lay around the bones.

A sick feeling rises up in your throat. When you turn, the man is still behind you. Only now he's hovering in the air.

Now you're certain this isn't Archie. Someone murdered this man. They boarded him up inside the wall. And his ghost wants you to know.

Before you can do anything, the room goes dark. You feel cold all over.

"Hello?" you say, but no one answers.

You feel your way forward, but there's a wall in front of you. You turn around and bump into another wall. You realize with horror you've been trapped inside the room where the man's body was found. You scream, but no one ever hears you. Your internship at the theater is going to last for all eternity.

THE END

To follow another path, turn to page 15.

To learn more about haunted theaters, turn to page 101.

"Excuse me, sir," you say. "Do you need any help?"

The actor stops pacing and glares at you. "That thief stole my best wig!" he exclaims, waving his cane like a dagger.

You ask who stole his wig. He tells you it was Thomas, a fellow actor. "He's in the lounge with it now! How dare he!" the man says.

Charles Macklin

“Let me speak with Thomas,” you say and hurry to the lounge.

It’s empty. You go back to the hallway, but the actor is gone. Suddenly, the sounds of a struggle come from the lounge. You hurry back inside to find the angry actor yelling at another man.

“You stole my wig, Thomas!” he shouts before swinging his cane at the man. The cane lodges itself in the other man’s eye!

You open your mouth to scream. But then a stagehand knocks on the door. The men vanish! Your whole body grows cold. You hold onto the wall to keep from fainting.

“I saw two men fighting,” you explain. “But they . . . disappeared!”

Turn the page.

The stagehand gasps. "You might have seen the ghosts of Charles Macklin and Thomas Hallam."

She tells you Macklin was a cranky actor who often performed at the Theatre Royal. He killed actor Thomas Hallam with his cane in 1735.

"Macklin's ghost has been spotted skulking around backstage," the stagehand continues. "It's as if his ghost can't find peace after the murder."

You're not sure what you just saw. But you're glad you didn't get on the bad side of Macklin's ghost.

THE END

To follow another path, turn to page 15.
To learn more about haunted theaters, turn to page 101.

You help the stagehand pick up the playbills. She thanks you. Then someone radios her on her headphones.

"Would you mind dropping these at the manager's office?" she asks. "I'm needed in props right away."

"I'd be happy to help," you say.

She gives you the playbills and directions to the manager's office. After a few wrong turns, you find the office.

"Hello?" you say and knock.

No one answers. The door is partly open. You slip inside and put the playbills on the desk. You're about to leave when a pen flies off the desk. It smacks the wall. Your heart races. You're the only person in the room.

Turn the page.

Before you can leave, a man enters. He wears a brown tweed suit. He opens a cupboard, digs around, and leaves again. He never even looks at you.

Must be the manager, you think. *Not very friendly.*

You leave the backstage area and head for the auditorium. It's time for your meeting with Archie. You find him waiting for you in the front row. He is definitely not the strange man in gray you saw in the lobby. You introduce yourself. You also mention your run-in with the cranky manager.

Archie looks at you strangely. "That doesn't sound like Helen," he says. "She's tough but kind."

"Who's Helen?" you ask.

Arthur Collins

"Helen is the manager of the Drury Lane," Archie says slowly. "Who did you see?"

You describe the man you saw. Archie leads you to a photograph on the wall. It's the man you saw! A plaque underneath reads: Arthur Collins, Drury Lane Manager from 1897 to 1923.

THE END

To follow another path, turn to page 15.
To learn more about haunted theaters, turn to page 101.

CHAPTER 5
HAUNTED THEATERS

"The show must go on."

This phrase has been uttered by those in the theater for hundreds of years. But for some, the show goes on even after death.

Many theater buildings are quite old. Thousands of performers, workers, and patrons pass through them every year. Some people have even died inside their walls. That doesn't mean they're haunted. Or does it?

Many theaters have stories of actors or crew members returning from the other side. Perhaps their spirits came back to the theater they loved. Or could it be that people just crave a good ghost story?

Over the years, many workers at the St. James Theatre claimed to have encountered Yuri. Jim Hutchinson said the ghost saved his life, twice. Once, Jim was about to fall off the edge of the stage. Yuri's ghost shoved him to safety. Another time, a beam fell on the stage while Jim was with his young son. Jim said Yuri pushed him out of the way and carried his son to safety.

No one at the Palace Theatre has actually reported seeing Judy Garland's ghost. But there have been stories of feeling her presence. Others have heard her singing.

Charles Macklin really did kill fellow actor Thomas Hallam at the Theatre Royal Drury Lane in 1735. Macklin was convicted but received only a fine. He served no jail time. The existence of his ghost isn't as easy to prove. An angry specter resembling Macklin has been reported backstage. And rumors swirl that the ghostly Man in Gray spotted on the balcony may be Hallam's ghost.

No one can say for sure if ghosts haunt the St. James, Palace, or Drury Lane theaters. But many people have reported cold spots, ghosts, flickering lights, and strange sounds. It could be faulty wiring or imaginations running wild. Whatever the reason, the possible hauntings add even more drama to these exciting places.

More Ghostly Encounters

Actor John Wilkes Booth shot and killed President Abraham Lincoln at Ford's Theatre in 1865. Some say Booth's ghost returned to the scene of the crime. Ghostly footsteps and laughter are often heard there. The lights turn off and on by themselves.

Ford's Theatre

The Academy Theatre in Ontario, Canada, is haunted by a ghost named Mary. Legend says Mary worked at the theater as a caretaker. One night, she fell down the stairs and died. Her ghost is said to pull pranks. It moves small objects, slams doors, and turns off the lights.

Frances Alda performed at New York City's Metropolitan Opera House in the early 1900s. She died in Italy in 1952. Shortly thereafter, people say her ghost returned to the Met. She would sit in the audience and mutter negative comments about the show. When the Met moved to a new building, the hauntings stopped.

Other Paths to Explore

Many theater buildings are old and drafty. Some have aging plumbing and worn-out electrical wiring. If you felt a chill or saw lights flicker while at a show, would you think it was a ghost? Or would you look for a more rational explanation?

Imagine you're the star of a show at a so-called haunted theater. Would you feel comfortable performing there? Let's say several people have died in the building. Would that make you more or less likely to work there? Why?

Workers really did uncover a skeleton at the Theatre Royal Drury Lane. Imagine what that experience must have been like for the workers. Would you have stayed and finished the job after finding bones? Why or why not?

Glossary

electromagnetic field (i-lek-troh-mag-NET-ik FEELD)—a field of force created by moving electric charges

intern (IN-turn)—a person working for little or no money to gain experience

legend (LEJ-uhnd)—a story passed down through the years that may not be completely true

medium (MEE-dee-uhm)—a person who claims to make contact with spirits of the dead

monologue (MON-uh-log)—a long speech by one character in a drama

paranormal (pair-uh-NOR-muhl)—having to do with an unexplained event that has no scientific explanation

rigging (RIHG-ing)—a system of ropes, cables, or chains that supports a theater's curtains, lighting, and backdrops

spirit (SPIHR-it)—the invisible part of a person that contains thoughts and feelings; some people believe the spirit leaves the body after death

vaudeville (VOD-vill)—a stage show that may include comedy, music, magic, and stunts

Select Bibliography

Hawes, Jason, Grant Wilson, and Michael Jan Friedman. *Ghost Hunting: True Stories of Unexplained Phenomena from the Atlantic Paranormal Society.* New York: Pocket Books, 2007.

Maitland, Hayley. "Murder, Musicals, and Royal Romance: The History of Drury Lane, London's Oldest—and Most Haunted—Theater. *Vogue*. vogue.com/article/the-history-of-drury-lane-londons-oldest-and-most-haunted-theater; Accessed July 26, 2024.

McGill, David. *Full Circle: The History of the St. James Theatre.* Wellington, New Zealand: Phantom House, 1998.

Ogden, Tom. *Haunted Theaters: Playhouse Phantoms, Opera House Horrors, and Backstage Banshees.* Guilford, CT: Globe Pequot Press, 2009.

"The Ghosts of St. James Theatre." Wellington City Council. wellington.govt.nz/news-and-events/news-and-information/our-wellington/2022/06/ghosts-of-st-james; Accessed July 26, 2024.

Viagas, Robert. "The Ghosts of Broadway." *Playbill.* playbill.com/article/the-ghosts-of-broadway-com-329561; Accessed July 26, 2024.

Read More

Carlson-Berne, Emma. *Ghost Hunters.* Minneapolis: Lerner Publications, 2024.

Collins, Ailynn. *Can You Escape a Haunted Cemetery?: An Interactive Paranormal Adventure.* North Mankato, MN: Capstone Press, 2024.

Peterson, Megan Cooley. *Aaron Burr's Ghost and other New York City Hauntings.* North Mankato, MN: Capstone Press, 2021.

Internet Sites

About Theatre Royal Drury Lane
lwtheatres.co.uk/theatres/theatre-royal-drury-lane/about-theatre-royal-drury-lane/

The Science That Explains Paranormal Activity
thescienceexplorer.com/the-science-that-explains-paranormal-activity-980

Why Do We See Ghosts?
popsci.com/story/science/ghosts-real-science/

About the Author

Megan Cooley Peterson is a children's book author and editor. Her book *How to Build Hair-Raising Haunted Houses* (Capstone Press, 2011) was selected as a Book of Note by the TriState Young Adult Review Committee. When not writing, Megan enjoys movies, books, and all things Halloween. She lives in Minnesota with her husband and daughter.